distorted colours
and
beautiful disasters

Miriama

Copyright © 2018 Miriama Pipi-Ngaronoa
All rights reserved.
ISBN: 9781727420166

DEDICATION

Dedicated to the readers who support my writing, the writers who inspire me to keep going and everyone in between who has been there for this journey; thank you.

PS.

If you think I'm writing about you, I probably am.

CONTENTS

1	LOSS	7
2	PAIN	91
3	LOVE	171
4	HOPE	257
5	TRUTHS	332
6	ABOUT: the book	413
7	ABOUT: the writer	414

@sincerelymiri via Instagram and this book.

;

distorted colours and beautiful disasters

LOSS

Miriama

"Dear Nanna,
I forgive you
And
I hope you
Forgive me too.
Love from, me."

"You don't realise
How inevitable
Death is until
It's already far
Too late."

Miriama

"I didn't tell you
That I loved you
The last time that
I saw you because
It wasn't meant
To be the last time
That I saw you."

"Our family tree
Has no roots
Without you."

Miriama

"My family may not be *broken*
But that doesn't mean we don't need *fixing.*"

"One day everything was okay and nothing was wrong
Then the next day came around and suddenly
Everything was wrong and nothing was okay."

Miriama

"I felt like I lost everything
When I lost you."

"And it hurts like hell
When I wake up and
I realise that you are
No longer here with us."

Miriama

"Losing you
Fucked me up
Way worse
Than what losing him
Did to me."

"You're my lifeline
But all you do
Is leave me."

Miriama

"I lost myself
Trying to
Find you."

"Sometimes the people you love
Can turn into the people you hate."

Miriama

"No one who loves you
Will treat you as if
They don't deserve you
And
No one who deserves
To be in your life
Will ever treat you
Otherwise."

"I miss the warmth that your body used to leave
On my bedsheets, now they feel like nothing but
Loneliness and it's all because they're empty
Without you and even when I get into bed
I'm just not big enough to fill them
The way we used to
You're gone now and I'm still trying to figure
It all out, life without you has turned me
Bitter and confused as my body lays cold
Under the blanket you brought me
For Christmas that one year, it's my favourite
Although it doesn't seem to keep me warm anymore
Much rather the opposite as you've left your mark
On my heart the way you left your mark
Across the wall right near my bed frame
We used to laugh about it all the time
And talk about how it got there in the first place
But I have since covered it up because
The look of it made me sick and only made me
Miss you even more than I already do
Without you, my bed isn't the only thing that
Feels empty, I feel empty too
I hate this feeling, it's killing me on the inside
And the cure is your smile except
You've been away for a while and
You don't love me the way you used to because
You found someone new to be close to
You don't need me anymore but
I never stopped needing you."

Miriama

"Yet another day
Seems to go by
Like yesterday
But this time
Feels a little
Differently
Because lately
You've been
Acting distant
And you
Haven't really
Smiled for me
And I'm not sure
If this means
We're over
Or is this
What they mean
When they say
That there is
Trouble in paradise
Will time help
To heal us
Or will the pain
Eat away
At you
And I."

"It took you a full nine months
To form my heart
And only took you seconds
To break it
Was it worth it?"

Miriama

"All I want to do
Is make you proud
But it's proving harder to do now
Since you're not around."

"Oh but darling, won't you stay?
Won't you stay a little longer?
At least until the evening arrives
And the sun falls from the sky
We can watch the moon rise
I think it's meant to be full tonight
I remember what that felt like
But lately we've been so distant
That not even a kiss from you
Would make me feel alright
Please stay though, won't you?
Don't leave me for her just yet
The sky is about to turn blue
I love it even more
When it starts to turn into shades
Of purple and pink, oh how pretty it is
I remember when you used to think
That I was pretty and when
You used to think I was even
Quite beautiful in your eyes
But that's not how things are is it?
Not anymore, at least I tried
I tried and tried again and
I screamed to the Gods that I loved you
As much as I could manage
It wasn't enough but not only that
It just wasn't good enough either
But I still loved you and
I always gave you my heart to hold
And I kept yours safe even
When you became cold towards me
Because nothing could've stopped me
From ever loving you."

Miriama

"You never did take me seriously
When I'd try and tell you
About how the way you
Were treating me made me feel
As if my feelings weren't valid
Enough for you to even consider
You pushed me away far enough
Now there is nothing
I have nothing left to give you
Because you've drained me
Of everything I had and now
I've had enough and finally
I've decided it's time for me
To leave, time to go
You had issues with past
Friendships and I understood it all
But I can't handle being blamed
For the way you make me feel
About myself and how
You make me feel about us
I'm sorry but I just can't take it
Not anymore and that's why
This had to be done
You should have listened to me
When I said that I'm not just anyone
I would have stuck by you
Through it all
And now you'll never
Find anyone like me."

"I drink coffee now
Since you've been gone
The first thing I reach for
In the morning
Isn't you anymore."

Miriama

"I had to lose him first
To learn my worth
And I don't regret it
Not one bit."

"If you start being true to your heart
Then perhaps it will lead you back to me
But beware because we have fallen apart
So many times before in the past
And I'm just not so sure anymore
If I'll still be here waiting for you
I'll do my best to be here
But I'm not making any promises
Just in case I have to break them
So let's just wait and see
If I'm where I need to be
And if you get here
You'll know where to find me
Please hurry though
Because I've waited such a long while
Almost all my life
For us to be together
And my forever is running out
And I'm running out of breath."

Miriama

"You pushed me away
Then begged me
To come back
Only to push me away
All over again
This time I left
All on my own
And you had the nerve
To question where I went
Yet you were the reason
Why I had to go."

"I wish you cared enough about me to leave
When you knew I didn't have the strength
To do it myself, it could have saved me
You could have saved me but you chose not to
You didn't hesitate to save yourself though
Good for you but you were never good for me."

Miriama

"You fill my glass
With vodka
I slip my pants off
And slide
Into the pool
I can tell
By the look
On your face
That the water is cold
Possibly freezing
But I cannot tell
Vodka fills my mind
And liquor
Runs through my veins
I am gone
But I still remain
You move closer to me
So I move
Further away
We begin to make plans
For our wedding
We even practice
A slow dance
To the song that will play
We talk of names
For the children
We will adopt
And have of our own
But
You are not him
And I am alone
Once again
It happens
Once more."

"Losing you permanently is what finally
Made me realise your significance to me
In the family, no one knew me like you."

Miriama

"And I still don't understand
Why He chose to take you away
Instead of me because we all know
It should have been me, it should've been."

"Sometimes I imagine that you are still here with me
I imagine that you are literally right beside me
And I have an entire conversation with you but
It hurts because I didn't get enough time with you
To get to know you and everything about you
I don't know what you'd really say for me to do
So I reply back with what I think you'd say
But it hurts because it just doesn't feel the same
I wish you were still around to tell me to
Clean up my room, have breakfast, let the light in
From the window in my room and before you left
I didn't listen but now that you're gone, I do
Just wish I listened when you were still here
When I had the chance to hear your voice
With my own ears instead of pretending to hear it
Inside my messed up head because now my mind
Is tangled with thoughts of you and thoughts
Of what you'd say to me if you could
But they don't ever come and they never will."

Miriama

"People hate you when you're sitting across from them
Or living across from them in different countries
And yet, the second you pass away and leave the earth
The waterworks start, the compliments and the emotions
Begin to kick in but I know the truth
No one ever really cares about you unless you're due
To be put in the ground."

"You were the fuel to the fire
The only one that could keep a family
Together when all they wanted to do
Was be apart from one another."

Miriama

"I know what he's thinking
He thinks I have a drinking problem
Of course, I don't
But if I did then I got it from her
And I don't want to let anyone
Take that away from me
Like He took her away from us."

"Please don't tell me that she is in a better place now
Because in my heart I know for a fact
That there is no better place for her than right here
With us so please save your condolences
Because I do not want them."

Miriama

"I never even thought about
What it would be like
To lose you because
I never believed that it would
Happen so soon and yet
I guess it's true when they say
That you don't always
Have enough time with the ones
You love and I guess that's why
You should make the most of it
If only I did because I know
For a fact that I didn't."

"It tears me up
On the inside
Sharing all of my
Thoughts and
Feelings with you
And anyone
Because it feels as if
Everyone in the world
Knows about you and I
And someone
Could so much as breathe
Your name
And the glue that I've used
To fill my wounds
Will crack
And I will break
All over again."

Miriama

"I just needed to see you one last time
To prove to myself that it was really over
And I was going pretty strong
Until I saw your smile and heard your voice
That's when it all came back to me
All of it like it had never left in the first place
And I knew already what was coming next
Because it's when I saw your face
The tears started to flow all over again
My heart breaking all over again
And there was nothing that I could do about it."

"Sometimes water
Is thicker than blood."

Miriama

"I think I lost
My mind
When I lost you."

"I hope that one day
You know what it feels like
To wait up all night
Waiting for a phone call
That is never going to come
To lie awake
Waiting for a text message
That never even got sent
I hope one day
You know what it feels like
To lose someone
That was never even yours
To begin with
Then and only then
Can you tell me
How I should feel."

Miriama

"She loved you, you know?
She really did, she loved you
She would've died for you too
And I guess in a way she did
But it didn't have to be like this
It didn't have to end like this
She loved you more than life itself
And now she has paid her debt
My only wish is for you to realise
You killed the girl who sold her soul
For a love that the devil wrote himself."

"I hope you die inside
Knowing you took away
From this world
The only person
That ever loved you."

Miriama

"She says something that makes sense
But when I see the look in her eyes
It doesn't because her eyes are drained
Of all emotion
She told me she was just tired
But I can tell she is absolutely exhausted
How can someone keep doing this
To the only person who could ever love them?"

"Your mental illness
Will never be an excuse
For the way you treat her
Don't even try it."

Miriama

"I lost my best friend
Because of you."

"Since she's been with you
I can't even remember the last time
That I saw her smile
Tell me what this says about you."

"I don't want to die
But if this is what
They call living
They lied
Because I can barely
Survive through
Another day."

"I don't see myself
Ever getting over
The loss of you
The death of you
Instead
It feels like I miss you
More each and every
Day that goes by
And I am without you."

Miriama

"There are so many questions
That I have for you
But they are only going to go
Unanswered
And knowing that is going to
Be the death of me."

"You never really know how long
You have left with someone
So don't wait a second longer
Tell the people in your life that you love them
Tell the people in your life that you care about them
Because every second counts and the longer you wait
The more time you'll lose to tell the ones
Who mean something to you that you love them
Say these things while they're still here
The last time I saw her I didn't tell her I loved her
And it wasn't meant to be the last time *but it was*."

"I think about you at night
When I wake up at 3am I think about you then too
I think about you all the time
I write about you all the time as well
When I'm driving home from work, I think about you
I imagine having conversations with you
In my head
I think about all the things
That we never got the chance to do together
I think about all the trips we planned
And I think about all the time I had here with you
That I didn't spend to tell you how much I love you
I think I will regret that for the rest of my life."

"Although I can't remember
I can't forget either
And I can't figure out
What's worse
Remembering everything
About you or
Not being able to forget."

Miriama

"Sometimes I want to die
Not because I can't live without you
But because I can't live with myself
After all I have done…"

"One day I was driving
And I had a flashback
Of you and I
In the hotel room that night
And my vision blurred
For just a few seconds
But when it came back to me
It felt like an entire
Eternity had gone by
All over again."

Miriama

"I wish I told you
All the things
That I didn't say
When you were
Still here but
Now all I can do
Is write them
All down
On pieces of paper
That will never
Find their way
To you."

"There is a house on top of a hill
Where I stay from time to time
There are lightbulbs in the lights
Switches for all the power points
Water ready to flow from the taps
Furniture waiting to be used
An oven waiting to cook a meal
A queen sized bed waiting to be filled
Photographs of a once happy couple
Line the corridor walls, framed
Almost but not quite, picture perfect
But nobody is home
And nobody is ever coming back."

Miriama

"Admitting that I miss you
Would mean admitting that you're
Not here anymore
And I'm just not ready to do that yet."

"I didn't want to lose you
But it happened anyway."

Miriama

"I don't have enough
Fingers and toes
To count just how often
I've lost my mind
Over you."

"But how can the person
That birthed you
Not even want to know you."

Miriama

"November 26th
The day you
Were taken away."

"I tried everything to keep a straight face
Not because I didn't want anyone to see me cry
And not because I didn't want anyone to see me break
But because if I reacted this way to you
Then it would mean that everything
People have been telling me about you
Would be true and I couldn't, I just couldn't
And then I saw them bring you out
I saw you laying there, still and cold
I heard your mother scream and sob
Watched as your sons knees hit the ground
When they saw you and I saw your daughters
Cry tears that they had never cried before
And I didn't break that day I saw all of this
I fucking shattered into a million pieces."

Miriama

"I was so desperate
Not to cry
That I bit down hard
On the inside
Of my mouth
I was so numb though
That I didn't even
Wince when I drew blood
I didn't care
When I began to taste it
Nothing could hurt me
Anymore after this
Not even my own pain."

"I didn't lose the best parts of me that night
You stole them, you didn't borrow them
With the promise of returning those parts back to me
You simply helped yourself to my body
With the mentality that you owned me
You did not have consent, you did not have permission
But you still made a decision to take what was not yours
There is a harsh word for someone who does that
Although I guess because you weren't able to succeed
It doesn't count for you but it does and one day
Reality will catch up to you and when it does
You will think of me and you'll wish you *stopped*
When I begged for you to *stop* and you didn't
And you'll regret it more than I ever could."

Miriama

"Losing you hurt like hell
But waking up every day
Without you feels worse."

"There are so many things that I wish I could say to you
But I can't, there are so many questions and I wish
I had the chance to ask you all of them but I can't
I'm so busy spending my days wishing for things
That will never happen without you here."

Miriama

"I loved you
And I still lost you."

"It's still so crazy to me
That you can spend weeks
Months, years
With someone and then
One day
They're not there anymore
Why does shit like this
Have to happen."

Miriama

"The journey to get to you
Felt longer than usual
It was clear as to why it felt like this
Usually we'd arrive with smiles
On each of our faces and yet
There was none of that at all
Instead it was the opposite
We had arrived to say goodbye
It was going to be the last time
We'd have the opportunity to do so
I wasn't ready, I'm still not
None of this makes sense
This isn't right
This is *not* how things are supposed to be."

"I wish I had more time with you
To become intoxicated on a Monday night
Tuesday afternoon, Wednesday morning
Thursday around lunchtime and Friday noon
The times I had with you, drunk or sober
Came to an end far too soon."

Miriama

"Sometimes I think that I'm going crazy
And it scares me
It also scares me to think about all the things
That I would easily do for you
Because there is literally nothing I wouldn't do
And it worries me
What if it isn't mutual?
What if the type of way that I feel about you
Isn't the same kind of way you feel about me
It wouldn't make sense but at the same time
It would be the only thing in this
Already fucked up world that would make sense
I would probably understand in some way
If you didn't feel the same
But I do know that you love me, I know you do
Because I see it in your eyes
And the way you act, I can't explain it
But I do know that you love me
If you didn't, you wouldn't be here
Especially not with me after all I've done to you
We both know I don't deserve you
Perhaps you don't deserve me either
But you chose to stay all while knowing
That you could have anyone you wanted
And you chose to be with me
You choose to be with me
And even though I wouldn't admit it entirely
I would never let you go
I just wouldn't be able to
How can you expect someone
To let go of the only person who has ever loved them
Doesn't seem fair to me
I hope that's a decision I never have to live through
I can't see myself without you
But I won't be begging for you to stay
If you wish to leave, you can
If you go, you go and if you stay then you stay
However if you decide to stay
Then please
Stay with me and not against me because

It's you and I against the world
Not you and I against each other
Fight beside me, with me and not against me
Help me make everything right again."

Miriama

"It truly is unfortunate
That it takes a tragedy
This extreme
To bring a family
Together."

"There's more chance of me
Losing you to work
Than losing you to a her
I can't decide
Which one would be worse."

Miriama

"When I die
I want to be made into ashes
Beautiful
Silvery
Ashes
I don't want to be scattered
In the ocean
Find a way to send me
Back into the sky
Where the rest of the stars are
Give me back to the universe."

"Tears poured as I saw you
Lowered into the ground
As we returned you to the earth
And I realised that I wasn't ready
But it was already too late
You were gone now, for good
And there was nothing
I could have done to stop it
From happening…"

Miriama

"The pain of my father
I see it in his walk

The pain of my mother
I see it in her smile

The pain of my family
It shows, crystal clear

We have lost someone
Dear to us all

The fire
That was once
Indestructible

Has been put out
By the tears
Of her friends
And her family

Her children
Finally
They come together
Like nothing ever
Happened

After years of silence
And drama
They are here
For her

Without her."

"I can't begin to describe how willing I was
To rip my own heart from my chest
So I could hand it over to you and bring you back
And yet I don't think I was the only one
Because I would've done that in a heartbeat."

Miriama

"I don't like being here
Without you
This shit isn't fair."

"Life and death
You don't have one
Without the other."

Miriama

"I'm still waiting for you
To show up out of the blue
Waiting and wishing
That you were still here."

"People say this all the time
But there is not a day that goes by
That I don't think about you
I don't know what to do anymore."

Miriama

"If I had one last chance
To ask you something
I would ask you for
Forgiveness."

"I didn't realise
I needed more time
Until it was already
Too late to be with you."

Miriama

"Loss can change
So many things
You'd be surprised
At who I used to be
Before you left me."

distorted colours and beautiful disasters

PAIN

Miriama

"They told me
Time heals all wounds
But pain is what healed mine."

"Drunk and confused
I needed you
But you had already
Left me behind
To go and be with
Somebody new
Because apparently
Anything else was
Better than being
With me even in my
Time of need."

Miriama

"Did you ever feel any shred of guilt?
When I told you what he did to me
Did you feel bad?
For leaving me behind

Drunk
Alone
By myself

I needed your help
I reached out to you
But you were already gone

Do you feel guilty?
On his behalf
Because when I said *stop*
He didn't *stop*

And when I asked
For your help
You didn't have any
To offer me."

"What kind of friend
Are you
To leave one of your own
Alone."

"I tried to forgive you
For what you did to me
But I couldn't bring myself
To forget his face
The one who didn't
Stop
When I said
Stop."

"You should have gotten rid of me
When you had the chance to."

Miriama

"My ribs crack
Beneath the pressure
Of your love
Is this what
All the fuss is about?"

"I broke my own heart
Being careful not to break yours."

Miriama

"You told me you loved me yesterday
I wonder what those words mean today."

"I have learned the hard way
That you treat me as if
I am disposable
Because you know
That I will
Never dispose of you."

Miriama

"How many other girls
Begged for you to *stop*
And you didn't?"

"Who was it that taught you
That *no* didn't mean *no*?
And *stop* didn't mean *stop*?
Who taught you to act like this
Or did you learn these things
All on your own…"

Miriama

"What he did to me was not my fault
And no one can tell me otherwise."

"You may have forgotten
All about me but
My experience with you
Will last me
An entire eternity."

Miriama

"I don't dare to ask if you think of me
I already know the answer
You think of me as often as I don't think of you
And I think about you all the time."

"I keep trying to wake up from this nightmare
But even I know
That some things are just impossible to reach."

Miriama

"As I sleep next to the man I love and whom loves me
I have nightmares about you and your hands
One covering my mouth and the other around my neck
When I wake from it and I'm shaking in my own skin
That doesn't really feel like my own anymore
I think about what would have happened if perhaps
You had killed me instead of leaving me
Cold and lifeless because ever since that night
I haven't felt the same and I don't feel sane anymore
And I only ever feel safe when I'm with him or my dad
When I think about what you did to me
I wonder what would have happened
If you had killed me yourself because ever since then
I've felt less alive and more like I'm dead
And I struggle every single day to get over what you did
I don't know how to tell those around me
What happened to me on a night that was supposed to be mine
The one night I decide to go out and try my best
To just have fun and forget everything that I had lost
In the past few months and I just wanted to feel good for once
And then this happens, you happened
But all you had to say was that *shit happens* and I guess
You're right but nothing in my life has ever felt so wrong
No one ever truly understands the fact that
When this happens, it stays with you forever
And it doesn't matter what I was drinking, wearing
Doing or saying because nothing could ever justify
What he tried to do to me, what he *did* to me
But how do you explain to the ones who love you
That this isn't what you intended, isn't what you wanted
How do you explain to the ones who love you
That it wasn't them that failed you
How do you explain that it was me who failed me
I failed myself, I should've done better for myself
And yet I didn't and I'll spend forever wishing that I did
Question is, will I still have him or will I be alone again?"

"It hurt the most
When you of all people
Blamed me
For what he did as well
As the entirety
Of society
I guess I believed
You'd be able to
See it differently
But I was wrong
About so many
Different things
You and him
Deserve each other
I hope you end up
Very happy together."

Miriama

"When you left
You didn't just
Take the air
Out of my lungs
But you took
With you
The words from
My heart that
I would use
To write down
My emotions
My feelings
My thoughts
Now instead
Of seeing them
On paper or
On a screen
All I see inside
Of me are the
Things that remind
Me of you
And I just
Want it all to stop
But we never get
What we want."

"It pained me
So much
To see you
Walk away
From me
But
It pained me
Even more
Because
I knew
There was
Nothing
I could do
To stop you
From leaving
All over again."

"You have been the cause
Of the harshest pain
I've felt in my life and yet
You show no sympathy
Or sign of regretting
What you have done to me
So I show no feeling or
Emotions at all anymore
All because of you."

"You hurt me
Then blame me for the pain

If I did
What you do to me

You would shoot me
Dead in the brain."

Miriama

"You never cared
Even though I did."

"I'm lost
Waiting to
Be found
But you
Have left
You have
Gone away
With someone
Else and
I am
Alone still
Waiting for
Someone to
Find me."

Miriama

"You promised to protect me from the world
But you couldn't even protect me from yourself."

"Family is meant to be everything
So why do I feel like nothing?"

Miriama

"What will you tell your daughter
When she comes home one day
With tears in her eyes and a broken heart
Her voice breaking as she tells you
All about the boy who shattered her soul
What will you tell your daughter
When she describes the things he did to her
That you once did to me
What on earth are you going to tell your daughter
If she goes through the same things
That you put me through but it doesn't matter
How much I hate you for it, I swear
I hope your future daughter
Never has to go through what you did to me."

"Your sober lips found my drunken ones
And you passed it off as a goodnights kiss
It woke me when I realised that you are not him
It shook me to my core when I realised
I did not say yes or give you consent to do this
I woke up and told you to *stop* but you didn't."

Miriama

"And it seems
That I always find myself
In the arms of men
Who don't seem
To really care at all
About me and
They only want to use me
And sadly I still let them."

"When you have me
You don't seem to want me
When I'm gone
You seem to need me
What's it going to be?
Make up your mind please."

Miriama

"The stars aligned for us
But the sun and the moon
Did not approve."

"I forgot
How to be
Happy
After
You left me."

Miriama

"How do you know
When you have killed?
What if
It is not when the heart
Stops beating
But when a heart
Becomes broken and
Irreparable
Based off of your actions
Because
Of what you said
In the past
Or in present time
Or what you have to say
In the future
It is all planned
Perhaps
When I left you
And it broke you
It was then
That I killed you."

"You put your arms
Around me
Pulling me closer to you
I breathe you in
But it doesn't feel right
You are not him
And you never
Ever will be."

Miriama

"It's like a battlefield
Between us
We hurt each other
In all kinds of ways
But we always
Find our way back
And come together
We can't live
Without each other
But we refuse
To live for
One another so
What's it going to be?
How long
Until we go too far?
How many times
Until it's one too many?
And I can't find a way
Back into your arms
And you can't
Find your way back
To my eyes."

"My son will always know
How to treat a woman
Even if his father doesn't.

My daughter will
Always know her worth
Even if her mother
Sometimes forgets her own."

Miriama

"I only ever needed
For you to become the man
That I needed
Because when you
Asked me
To become the woman
You needed
I did
I just wish that you knew
How to give back
What you receive."

"And sometimes I wish
People cared more
I wonder what it feels like
To have someone
Who cares about me
The way that I care
About you
If only I knew, oh
If only."

Miriama

"Your silence and isolation
Are the only two things
I remember about you."

"If I'm being completely
And utterly honest
I long for our twisted romance
To become an uncomplicated
Reality."

Miriama

"We weren't made for each other
I wasn't the one for you
And you weren't the one for me
But we fought like hell
To be together even when we
Both knew that it would never
Work out the way we hoped."

"The words to the lie
I'm about to tell
Leave my lips before
I am able to
Stop myself."

Miriama

"I cut the tips of my fingers
Picking up your broken pieces
You didn't do anything to help me
Said nothing either
You let me bleed out and let me
Die trying to keep you alive."

"I'm sorry for blaming you
For all the things
I was doing wrong

I'm sorry for hurting you
Saying the things I said
It was wrong of me

A mistake I will regret
For as long as I live

Forgive me
I'm sorry
For the pain
That I have caused

At your expense
All because I was upset
With no one else
But myself

Let me hold you
In my arms
Take the pain away
From me please

I was wrong
You were right
I know this now

Tell me
That I have time
To make things right
To tidy the mess
I made

Tell me that everything
Will be okay for us."

Miriama

"You picked me up and carried me
Away from the pain
Shielding my heart from the loss
That I had just experienced
But then you left
And it went back to the way
It was before
You came into my life
Only it was worse."

"I hope one day
You look back
And realise
All the pain
And hurt
You have caused
Me
And I hope
You hurt
More than
I ever could."

"Memories of you haunt me
In my dreams and during the day
Flashbacks hit me and it feels like
I wake up from a nightmare
Almost every morning
I cared about you and
Maybe it's my own fault
That I got hurt the way I did
Because I was silly enough
To let you back in
Every single time you came
Knocking at my door."

"It hurts me to think
That I never really did
Mean anything to you."

"It's sad to think about when I look back
On you and I
Because it seems that you knew
How much I was hurting to be with you
You knew I'd never leave you
Instead of doing the right thing
Like you'd always promised to do
You couldn't even bring yourself to leave
Even when you knew
That staying would cause me
Even more pain than you actually leaving
And don't bother trying to say
That you stayed because you loved me
Because we both know
That you stayed because of the way
I made you feel and it had nothing
To do with how you felt about me
But everything to do with how I was able
To make you feel about yourself
You tried to isolate me on purpose
Wanting me to depend on you
More than anything and even
When I did, all you did was turn away
You didn't stay because you loved me
You stayed because you loved
How it felt to have someone like me around."

"I hate feeling like everything is my fault
But at the same time I guess I wouldn't
Feel this way if everything wasn't my fault
So maybe it is."

Miriama

"I begged you to stay
Told you my fears
About how
I'm scared to be alone
But you left anyway."

"I think the worst kind of heartbreak
Is done by the one who promised
That they would be different than the rest
Then turned out to be exactly the same
And even worse than anyone before
Had ever been towards you."

Miriama

"I promised that I would be honest
I'm not one to wish hurt or harm or pain
On anyone but even still
You're not just anyone and I don't wish
For you but I hope that you do
Find out what it really feels like
To be hurt over someone who
Doesn't give a fuck about you."

"There was nothing poetic
About the way you broke my heart
Until I started writing about it
Then instead of falling apart over it
I was able to make art out of it."

Miriama

"I don't think the pain
I feel over you
Is every going to go away."

"The heaviness of the pain your loss brings me
Is enough to knock me down onto my knees
Sometimes I am able to get up and continue to walk
Other days I find myself paralysed and numb
Unable to move, unable to think, unable to do anything."

"I feel like I'm drowning
In happiness but I can still breathe
What's wrong with me?"

"I tried to forget you
And there are even days where
I don't even think about you
But then there are those nights
Where all I can do is wonder
All about you
Those are the nights
That I lose the most sleep
Over you and I just want it
To end, I need it to end."

Miriama

"I tried to stick by you
But it's gotten to the point
Where I can no longer
Support your decisions
So in turn
I had to make my own
Even the ones that hurt
And left me all alone
It's too late
To regret them now."

"I feel like I was robbed
But then I guess it wasn't
Really a robbery because
I chose to let you in
Maybe I'm just another
Victim of a fraud."

Miriama

"We get used to the pain
We think we deserve."

"The beginning of the end is always the worst
Part of everything
The aftermath of the ending
Is the hardest part of all
Leaving you has left me broken and sore
One day I hope to know
That it was the only chance I had
At surviving on my own
Life without you was hard at first
Since then I've learned to accept
Things for what they are
I've since learned to accept people for who they are
The good and the bad
The ugly and the sad
Parts of us that no one
Has ever seen or ever will see
Haunt us if we don't let them out
Don't be like me and learn the hard way
Because after that nothing is ever the same."

Miriama

"I want to walk directly into the sun
And burn myself alive
That way every time you look up to the sky
I will be there
Looking down on you as you stare
I want to live on the dark side of the moon
But still shine bright enough
To bring light into your room at night
When you least expect me
Haunting you in your sleep
Forever and always
In your dreams."

"I don't ever want to be alone
And yet I always find myself alone and lonely
Missing you as always
Craving your arms around me
You're the only one that has what I need
But the only thing you're good at
Is leaving me."

Miriama

"I don't remember
A time in my life
When I didn't feel
Anything but numb
I've always been like this
I've always felt this shit."

"I know what's wrong with me now
I care too much because no one else ever cares enough
I spend too much time fixing what's broken around me
To realise that I just need to focus on me, myself and I
This shit will be the death of me, I just wish people
Knew how to care about me the way I care about them."

Miriama

"You can always
Find a way
To forgive
But you can never
Find a way
To forget
And I hope you never forget what you did to me."

"I'm falling and fading away
Into the darkness, into the abyss
No one can save me now
Not even Him
I'm going, going; gone."

Miriama

"You took a lot out of me
Right before you left
You emptied me of everything
That made me; *me.*"

"The mask I wear, the smile on my face
It's all fake
But no one knows it except me

They call me a writer, they call me poetic
When all I'm doing
Is a form of self-expression
To keep the demons away from me
When things get too depressing

There are cracks that are starting to show
They are no longer invisible
The tears are ready to pour

Similar to the way I spill the words
Into every piece
I let everything go in every single word
The more I do, the better I feel
But that doesn't stop the bad
From creeping back over
Taunting my every move

As if one wrong move
And I'll be gone
The sad thing is

I'm already dead."

"Pain has not been the cause of the scars
That cover my body, people have."

"I watched the forever you promised me
Burn and turn into ashes
Disappearing into the wind
While you were hiding in the background
Sneaking around with her."

"You didn't mean anything you said
Not even when you said you cared."

"All I wanted was for you to listen to me
You said you were but you weren't hearing me
I just needed you to fucking be there for me."

Miriama

"I have this weird tendency
To ruin everything
That's ever been good for me."

"My heart wasn't the only thing you left broken
You left me, shallow and empty
How do I survive on my own
When you're the only reason I was alive
In the first place?
This is so easy for you, teach me
Show me how
I don't want to care anymore, tell me
How do you not care about me anymore?
There is no difference
Between emptiness and loneliness
Because they both involve you being absent."

"Everything
Feels
Numb."

"We fell apart because you were trapped
Somewhere in the past."

Miriama

"It hurt me to think
That you thought
I could never be
The one for you
When all along
You've been
The one for me. "

LOVE

Miriama

"City lights
Flashing by
I look to you
And I see
Stars forming
Where your eyes
Used to be
After all of this
Do you still
Love me
As much as you did
When you first
Met me?"

"Set the mood right
Tonight
We are going to go
And make love
Under the stars
Under the bright
Moonlight."

Miriama

"I counted the stars tonight
I asked them each if I was going to be alright
They sparkled twice in unison
And I whispered back, *well alright then*
I knew that I could trust them
So I closed my eyes and made one last wish
And hoped I'd see you tomorrow
To give you one last kiss
Before it was time for you to go."

"I pray
That we are more
Than the love
We make."

Miriama

"Isn't there something beautiful about us?
In the way
That no matter how far apart we feel or become
From each other
We always find a way back together
As if it isn't enough that even the people
Around us disapprove entirely of me and you
I guess we're the lucky ones
Who have fate on our side
I won't lie but we're obviously special
In a sense, it's as if the universe seems to tell us
Stop splitting in two
Because you were made as one."

"You've always been
Everything that I've
Ever needed and more."

Miriama

"Love is everything
You are everything
My everything."

"You are all I need
All that I've ever wanted
And all that I could ever care for
It's you, it's always gonna be you."

Miriama

"I loved you then
I love you now
I love you always."

"I wish you
Love and happiness
Among other
Beautiful things
Life has to offer
Even if
I am not part
Of the plan
God has for you."

Miriama

"My body is your canvas
Paint me with your lips."

"There is something wrong with me
Deep down
Perhaps it is the way that
I love you too much and not enough
All at the same time."

Miriama

"I promise
To love you
Even if you don't
Love yourself
Even
If you don't
Love me
Anymore."

"Call me baby
And when you tell me
You love me
Mean it."

Miriama

"I whispered your name
To the moon and
The entire earth shook
With disapproval
But even still
I continued to love you."

"Be with someone who
Makes you happy
Accepts you for you
And someone who
Will love you
Through it all
Through everything
This is someone
Who you can be proud
To be with forever."

Miriama

"Everything I do
I do for me
I do for you
I do all of this for us."

"I wish I could tell you
In my own words
Just how much you mean
To me but each time I try
The words
That I'm looking for
I'm never able to find and
I can't describe any of it."

Miriama

"Embrace me
Hold me tight
Don't let go
Just one
More night."

"Sometimes the love
You have to give
Is enough but also
Too much
At the same time
Instead of filling up
The other
It often leads to
Suffocating them
Until they can
No longer breathe
And that's how I learned
That even love
Can turn into pain."

Miriama

"And I always
Keep my promises
When I say
Forever
Then I mean forever
Because if I ever
Said it then I meant it."

"You are the muse to outdo all other muses
You are the music my soul listens to
The rhythm to the beat of my heart
The colour of the sky during the day and at night
Especially when the stars are out
I see the reflection of galaxies in your eyes
Beautiful and magical
If it were to be the only thing I would see
For the rest of my life
I would be okay with that
There is no one else I would rather have
By my side than you."

Miriama

"I could have the world
On a silver platter
But if I don't get to
Share it with you
Then it won't matter
And I don't want it."

"Baby, we are so close
So fucking close
It's not too late for us
We will be able to start over again
We will be together again
I promise you
We are almost there
They said we wouldn't make it
But look at us now
Don't you see baby
We can do this
We are doing this
This is all us
The darkness has been scary
And frightening
But there is light at the end
Of this tunnel that leads us to Heaven
Our very own Heaven
Just you and I
The sun, the moon and the stars
Because that's all we need
Survival is possible
With you next to me
But I can't do this without you
Take my hand
We are almost there
Let me lead the way
I promise we will be alright
You will be okay
We're going to make it
Anything that stands in our way
You know I'm ready to fight it
Together we are unstoppable
Unbreakable
Untouchable
We are perfect
But only if we're together
I promise
You will be safe in my arms."

"He talks of death as if it is coming for him next
He is haunted by the nightmares he has
Almost every night
But he is still so happy and playful
You wouldn't think
He goes to sleep scared of what may come
For him during the night
I wish I could tell him that dreams are just dreams
But one day they will become a reality
And I think that scares me more than it scares him
Because one day I won't be here
I won't be able to see him play
I won't be able to see him grow into a young man
One day I won't be here to be able to care for him
The way I have been all these years
He's young and still finding it a little hard
To understand what death means completely
But I swear I'm going to do all I can
To make sure he isn't left here all alone
This world is too cruel for someone so kind
I want to promise that I will never go
That I will never leave
But I don't know how much time I've got
Before it comes for me
Before it's my time to leave
But I will always be here
Even when I'm not around anymore."

"Don't go looking for love
When you are ready, it will find you."

Miriama

"Don't get me wrong
Seeing you happy
Makes me happy but
Not as much
As it would if I
Was the one behind
That smile of yours."

"I don't care where we go
Or where we end up
As long as I've got you
Right by my side
I know for sure
I'm going to be alright."

Miriama

"You and I were nothing
But a brief love affair
That should never have
Lasted as long as it did."

"I've never felt the way I feel about you about anyone else
Except for myself because as I got older I learned
That in order to be able to accept the love I deserve to have
I needed to be able to give that love to myself first."

Miriama

"And even when I stopped believing in myself
You never did and I guess that's what made all of this
A hell of a lot easier than what it could've been like
If I was alone and without you but you proved yourself
You came through for me and that means everything."

"I think I loved you
Almost immediately
As soon as I saw you
Then I got to know you
And I *still* loved you."

Miriama

"It took some time
For us to realise
That you and I
Are in this together
And I really would
Not have it any
Other way."

"There is no one I would rather spend
A lazy Sunday with more than you."

Miriama

"I can't help but think about those times
That you would tell me you don't know what love is
I'd always think to myself *but how, but why*
Because how can you not know what love is
When I'm standing right in front of you."

"We both had to change and allow
For each other to grow apart
In order to be able to grow together
It wasn't easy, we knew that already
But it was the best decision
That we ever made and I'm just glad
Because even to this day
We still feel the same way."

Miriama

"You turned the love I gave you into pain
Pushed me away, told me to go
Then asked me to stay; *what do you want?*"

"You taught me
How to love
The ocean and
The sound of waves
And now I spend
Every summer day
At the beach
Waiting for you
To join me
Once again."

"His apologies come wrapped in my favourite
Home cooked meals, a candle-lit bubble bath
Apologies with a hint of mint in my lemon tea
He doesn't know how to say the words *I'm sorry*
But he does know how to show that he is
You taught me the most about the truth in
Actions speak louder than words
Your actions scream *I love you* and *I'm sorry*
Even if your words sometimes turn mean
Your actions will always be enough
For me to forgive you for whatever it is
That you may have done."

"I was so focused on loving you
That I forgot to love myself
I realised too late
That you were not capable
Of giving back what you received
Reciprocation is not something
You've ever been good at."

Miriama

"Don't call me a week later
And ask me why I haven't called you
Why I haven't texted you
Because you know why
Don't call me a week later
Talking about how I'm having fun
Without you because you're damn right
I am having fun without you
Don't call me a week later
Trying to apologise
Because it doesn't mean anything
Even if you fake cry
So don't call me a week later
When you realise
What kind of mistake you made
I won't be here
And you know why."

"Don't keep me around for company
Be with me because you need me
Because you love me."

Miriama

"Learn to reciprocate
What your partner gives."

"I knew how you felt about me
And I took advantage of that
When I shouldn't have
You knew how I felt about you
And you did the same thing
That I used to do
Is this really what we've come to?"

"It's amazing
What a good morning text
Can do for you."

"You have inspired
Almost every piece of writing
I have ever written."

"I wish I knew how to tell you that I love you
Without saying the words
I wish I knew how to let you know that you're everything
I have ever wanted and more, without saying the words
I wish I knew how to tell you that no one has ever loved me
The way you do without having to say the words
I wish I could say all of these things in such a way
That you'd really know what I'm trying to say
If only there was a way for me to turn the thoughts in my head
Into words that can do the feelings of my heart justice
I want so badly for you to know all of the thoughts
I have of you in just one day, often it becomes difficult
To focus on anything else as all I can ever do is wonder about
You, you, *you*
Ever since I met you, you've always been in my head
Ever since then; how am I supposed to focus?
How am I supposed to concentrate when the only thing
I'm worried about is you, *my love.*"

"I've never liked to call you and I a love story
But it is our story and we did fall in love along the way
So perhaps it is after all; a love story and of course
What kind of story would it have been
If we did not fall in love? Maybe not a story after all
I used to think that the timing was so wrong for us
And that's when I realised that I was wrong
The timing was not wrong for us
We were just wrong for each other, *at the time*
We were young, stupid and mad with love for each other
And we weren't quite sure how to execute
The way we felt but we did our best and that's what mattered
It mattered because that's what got us here
Where we are right now and I haven't told you this yet
But I'm so proud of us
I'm so proud of how far we have come as individuals
And as a couple, I don't give you enough credit
For what you do for us even though I know I should
I'm so lucky and thankful to have you, you, *you.*"

Miriama

"If it weren't for you
I wouldn't even have a muse."

"You helped me learn
That change is inevitable
And bound to happen
But also that it could be
A good thing
Even if it doesn't
Feel that way at first."

Miriama

"You'd ask me all the time
What's wrong with me?
I would tell you simply
*The only thing wrong with you
Is that you are not him.*"

"I remember the night we laid out near the pool
Drunk off of liquor that neither of us could afford
The sky was both dark and bright due to the stars
I counted them but lost count a few times
And I had to restart all over again
But it didn't bother you or me, thanks to the whiskey
I confessed my love for the moon and you looked over
With a confused look on your face
Before your smile arrived, I noted in my head
That sometimes it's late to the party
I told you I wasn't kidding about being in love
With the moon and you laughed and said *I know*
We drank more whiskey and practiced a slow dance
For our wedding, picking out all the songs to play
We were drunk off of an illusion
That alcohol tends to give those who drink too much
And love too little
Although it felt real, we both knew it could never be
You were not him and I was not her."

Miriama

"She smelled of watermelon wine, whiskey and vanilla
She looked like a mermaid, drunk off of salt water
And I prayed to whatever God is up there
That maybe one day she could be mine
Even if it was only for a few moments in time."

"I don't ever
Want anyone else
To know what it's like
To be loved by you
It's all mine, it's mine."

Miriama

"I can't help but love you
I once tried not to
And even after all of that
I find myself
Still loving you."

"All I ever wanted to do was love you
It was supposed to be a good thing
But you turned it into something horrible
Like I said, *I only ever wanted to love you.*"

Miriama

"The most unfortunate thing about love
Is that sometimes it's not enough
And I don't know what hurts more
Loving someone who cannot accept it
Or loving someone who doesn't even want it."

"I would wait forever
If it meant I got the chance
To get to know you
All over again."

"I loved you enough to stand by you
Through it all
Through every single fucking little thing
All the venom you'd spit during arguments
Over shit that didn't mean anything
I loved you enough to stand by you
And take care of everything to do with us
I loved you enough to lie for you
Loved you enough to feed bullshit
To those closest to me, those who loved me
I loved you enough to stay with you
After half the tricks you pulled
And all the games you played
To sneak around and get away with it
But right now, looking back
I wish I loved myself more
Than I could have ever loved you."

"You loved me enough to stand by me
Through everything
The lying, the cheating, the fighting
And I thought twice
About writing this because it hurts
My heart to think about it
But I need to say thank you
Not for loving me and sticking by me
But thank you
For letting me prove to you
And the rest of the world
That I can be a good person too."

"You're my favourite
Person in the entire world
And I wouldn't have it
Any other way."

"There is nothing
Traditional about us
At all."

Miriama

"You're *the one for me*
And I'm *the one for you.*"

"I thought we had something different
I thought we had something better than the rest."

Miriama

"I've never thought about my future without you in it
And I don't plan on it
Everything I do now in the present
Has always been for a future of you and I."

"Learn to take care of yourself first
Before you take care of anyone else
Learn to love yourself first
Before you love another."

"My prayers were answered
When I asked to have you
Saved for me."

"I may not be
What you need
But neither
Is she."

"Nobody gonna love me
Better than I can love me."

"How can I believe
That I was born to die
When you make me feel so alive?"

Miriama

"Allow yourself
To fall in love
With love making."

"T o u c h M e

The way I touch myself
To the thought of you
Late at night

W a t c h M e

As I lay it all out for you
Flaws n all
This is all for you

H e a r M e

Say your name
Or should I scream it
That depends on you

F e e l M e

And the way
My body
Will move for you."

Miriama

"And I know for a fact, if it weren't for you
I wouldn't even be here but how do I thank you
For doing all the things you do for me, for us
How do I show you how appreciative I am of you
I'll give my life to you, dedicate everything to you
At the end of each day this is all for you either way."

"Tell me everything
You want from me
Even if you think
It's impossible
Tell me everything
I can do for you
Endlessly
Spending eternity
Giving you exactly
What you need
Hopefully it will be
Forever you and me."

"And every year brings a new beginning
I guess that's why we chose for every NYE
To be our anniversary and I guess because
For the last four years we have been together
Drunk and in love it's the perfect date
For us to celebrate and I can't wait
For all the more new years to come."

"I love you but now
Things have changed
And I love you still
But only
In a different way."

Miriama

"No one has ever loved me
The way you do, as much as you do
I'm so lucky."

"I never liked Christmas
Until you came along
Now we celebrate it
As early as October and
Each year that passes
And we are together
On Christmas, I thank
All of my lucky stars
To have been blessed
With you."

Miriama

"He hurt you and what he said hurt you
What he did hurt you and pissed you off
But broke you? No way
My darling, you come from a long line
Of women who cannot be broken
We cannot be broken, we refuse to be broken
This will not break you and I will not let it
You cannot let this damage you in any way
It was him and not you
And you don't need to go looking for pain
When you have so much love around you
Just remember that you cannot be broken
No matter what anyone does or says to you
There is no one in this world
Who has the power to break you unless
You let them...

Words to live by, thank you Nanna."

"You want to know how I know your parents love you?
Because they didn't let me win when I wanted you
All to myself
You want to know how I know your mother loves you?
Because she went against me, her mother
So that she could be yours and that's how I know
She loves you
You want to know how I know your father loves you?
Because even though he didn't say a single word
I know that he was broken on the inside over you
If I had taken you from them, it would've killed him
I think that's why he would die for you
That's how I know he loves you
Don't you ever question your parents love for you
They show it in other ways, they don't always say it
But they love you, trust me they do
Because they didn't let me win, they fought for you
And these are the things that happened
When you were a baby that you don't know but I do
That's how I know they love you."

Miriama

*"I tried everything I could think of
I wanted to have you all to myself
This is how much I loved you
I was willing to hurt my own daughter
To get you
And maybe that wasn't the right way
To go about things but
Your Nanna loved you so much
And still do
I would've killed to have you."*

"Anytime I find myself questioning my worth
I look back on the times I had with you
And think of all the things you said to me
Whenever I need a reminder of who I come from
And where I come from
I think of all the wise words you shared with me
Makes it hard to think that I'm worthless
When I hear your voice telling me
All the things that I need to hear when I'm feeling sad

You don't need anyone else
To pick you up and dust you off
Because you can do that yourself
You do not need anyone else

Whenever I need a *gentle* reminder
I listen to your voice and it makes me really happy
And glad that I got everything you said to me
Captured in recordings because even though
You're not here anymore
Whenever I need you, *I have you*
And lately I've been needing more of you
But this is as good as it gets and until
We meet again, this is good enough."

Miriama

"And I still think your mother loves you
More than I ever could
So it would've been really selfish of me
To take you away from her
To take you away from someone who loves you
More than I ever could."

"The last time I saw you
You cried in my arms
And you told me you don't feel
As if you are good enough
I had to go and was in a rush
So I didn't get to ask you
Much about what you meant
When you had said that
And on the way back to my place
I cried all the way there for you
Because I didn't understand
How you could feel that way
When I love you so much
And I wondered what happened
Along the way and
Where I had gone wrong
To ever get to a point where you feel
As if you are not good enough
Because you always have been
Always will be."

Miriama

"You are loved
More loved
Than you will
Ever know

A gentle reminder from my Nanna to me
And *from me, to you."*

HOPE

Miriama

"I hope for the best because I deserve the best
And I hope the best for you
Because you deserve the best too."

"I fell in love with myself when it became clear
That you were never going to."

Miriama

"I hope you find whatever it is you are searching for
And I hope that whatever it may be
Is good for you and so much more
Than what you are expecting it to be."

"If you're looking for a sign
To do something
This is it."

Miriama

"Don't live your life setting limits and boundaries
For yourself, instead live your life
Believing that you can do anything you put your mind to
If you are truly able to believe in yourself
And what you love then you will never fail."

"There are people watching films
Making love for the first time
Opening mail with the heading of
I miss you
Cooking noodles with
Organic spices and red sauces
Buying lemon detergent
Ignoring *do not smoke* signs
Painting murals of his lips
In abandoned warehouses
Chewing the words
I love you
Over and over again, swallowing
Phone numbers and forgotten birthdays
Eating strawberry pies
Drinking white wine off of each other
Others open mouths
Ignoring the telephone
Reading this poem…

Somewhere
Someone is thinking
I am alone
Somewhere
Someone finally understands
They never really were."

Miriama

"Repeat after me;
I am strong
I am powerful
I am beautiful
I am in control
I am me and I am great."

distorted colours and beautiful disasters

"You are special, unique and beautiful
You will make it out of this dark fog
You are going to do amazing things
You will be okay, I promise you will be."

Miriama

"There is nothing on this earth or in this world
That you cannot do if you just put your mind
And your heart to it, you will go so far
I can already see it."

"*I'm not broken over you anymore*
And even as I said the words
In my head
When I said them out loud
Everything began to make sense
This happened for a reason
Not because I deserved it
But instead because I needed
To learn from this and finally say
*I'm not broken over you anymore
And mean it.*"

Miriama

"No one knows what the future holds
I'm not too bothered
As long as I've got you then I know
Everything is going to be alright."

"None of you believed that I would get as far as I have
It's okay, I'm not mad at any of you for that
Because if it weren't for any of what you'd say to me
I wouldn't be where I am to this day
I found strength and motivation underneath your hate."

Miriama

"God has blessed you with a heart too heavy to carry
The weight of the world is upon your shoulders
Because He believes you are strong enough
For this world and that, my darling you are
Although sometimes the darkness can overshadow
Your shining light and although you may stop
Believing in yourself yet no one else does
You feel alone in a world full of people
Who are just like you
Yet so different and uniquely beautiful in their own right
You are pure perfection in your own way
But the world is heavy and so is your heart
Heavy with sadness and you feel as though
Everything is falling apart and so are you
But you are wrong because you are
One of the strongest people I know and this world
And the people on it, *will not break you*
There are days where you think it may but
I will not let it
You are too precious for this world but
He has blessed us with you
And we are so lucky."

"Even the strongest hearts
Have cracks from broken pieces
Show now and then
Don't let this make you believe
That you are weak
Because you more than anyone
Have the strength to carry on."

"A letter to my future self;
I hope by now you have realised that
All you need to do is
Breathe
I promise everything is going to be okay
Some days it seems as if this will never end
But it does and you should be proud
Of how far you have come
The things you have achieved and accomplished
After everything you've felt and seen
For yourself, you deserve all of this
Believe it or not but you worked hard for this
This is what you get for doing your best
I hope by now you have realised that
All you need to do is
Listen
To yourself and learn to trust yourself
You know what you're doing and whatever it is
It's the right thing to do if you truly believe so
Keep pushing to become a better version of yourself
You are in control and the only person
Who can change your life is you so don't wait
For anyone else to do that for you
Take control, do what you gotta do
To get to where you want to be
And let the rest follow your lead and always
Remember that no matter what happens
Everything will work out and everything
Including you, is going to be okay."

"Please take care of yourself
If not for you then please
Do it for me."

Miriama

"Remember to enjoy the little things
Even when it seems like everything
Is falling apart because the little things
Will always find a way to make you smile
And help you get through the night."

"And I can only hope you find the faith
You need to get through the day
If it helps just remember
That I believe in you and I always will."

Miriama

"It gets easier, I promise
I wouldn't lie to you
I know sometimes
It feels as if things
Will never get better
Sometimes it feels
Like the light
At the end of the tunnel
Has disappeared and
Gone away but it hasn't
It's there
You just have to find it
Believe in yourself
You will get through this."

"A note to my past self;
Well, well, well. Look what we have here
Look at how accomplished you are
After all these years of looking at yourself in the mirror
And saying you'll never amount to anything
Well I told you so, didn't I tell you?
Now be proud of yourself, you've done everything right
Even if along the way
Sometimes it didn't feel like it
But you've always done everything that is best for you
That's important and isn't easy to do often
And yet you managed just fine
I wish I had known what you were going to go through
Before it happened
And I wish I could've done something to stop it
But if none of that happened
Then you wouldn't be the woman you are today
So let's not undermine what you've gone through
Because you got through it with or without help
You did it
No matter how difficult life got
You always managed to find a way out
Please be proud of yourself
Learn to love yourself more
Care for yourself and look after yourself more
And remember that if it weren't for everything
That happened you wouldn't be
Where you are right now and you wouldn't be
The person you are today
You have every right to be proud
Of the woman you have become
Right now is a good time to be alive
So let's make the most of it. "

"I hope you find inner peace
You deserve it."

"It doesn't cost anything to be nice to others
And kind to those around you
So why aren't we doing this more often?"

Miriama

"I hope you find someone who makes you happy
And I hope this person is everything you've ever wanted
Everything you've ever needed in your life
I hope you find someone who loves you for you
And I hope this person accepts you for who you are
Because you deserve someone who does."

distorted colours and beautiful disasters

"No matter what happens
Hope is *always* on your side."

Miriama

"You didn't give me a choice
You made a decision
And left me to lay in it
I hope you're happy with this."

"I lost hope for myself
The day I lost you
To someone else."

Miriama

"I hope that by the time
My kids are born into this world
It is a much better place
For them to call home."

"I hope that one day
I can make you all proud
But until then
This is all I have to offer."

Miriama

"You said that you would never be able
To love somebody like me
And I said that's okay because
I love myself enough to be without you."

"I hope you find happiness in everything you do
Because it's exactly what you deserve and more."

Miriama

"Still searching
For a better day
I hope I find it
Soon before
It's too late."

"I tried everything to get over you
Everything except hope even though
That's what got me through."

Miriama

"I hope you find a love that engulfs you
And fills your entire being that it becomes
The essence of who you are
 I hope when you find this love
That it wasn't at the hands
Of someone else and in fact
It's at the hands of yourself
Because self-love is more
Important than we believe."

distorted colours and beautiful disasters

"Honestly
I hope one day
You realise
What it's like
To miss someone
Who isn't yours
Anymore."

Miriama

"I hope that someday soon
You learn to love yourself
As much as I love you."

"I always had such high hopes
For you and I
I wanted badly to be your queen
But you couldn't even
Treat me like a human being."

Miriama

"I still find myself
Hoping and praying
That instead of you
It was me because
I still feel like
It should've been me
This entire time
And not you."

"I hope you never know
What it feels like to miss someone
Badly enough to lose your mind
To lose what's left of your sanity
Because trying to describe that
And the pain that comes with it
I cannot, I am not able to
So I hope you never know
What that's like."

Miriama

"In order to love myself
I needed to get to know myself first
And it wasn't easy
But it could've been worse
Coming to terms with the person
That I *used to be*
Was by far the most difficult thing
I've ever had to do
But I had this feeling in my gut
The entire time
That it was the right thing to do
And now I am
Where I am right now
And I wasn't happy yesterday
But I'm feeling happy today
I know I won't be happy every day
And that's okay
Because as long as I'm doing
What I love the most
Nothing can take away the hope
I have in my heart."

"I worry a lot
I don't know why
And I don't know how to stop
I've tried
I try all the time
But to not worry
Feels like trying to stop caring
And if I cared about you once
Then chances are
That I'll care about you always."

Miriama

"I cared about you so much, enough to try and save you
But it took me almost forever to realise
That there is no hope left in your eyes, in your life
I had to leave you, let you be and try hard to believe
That one day you will be okay, it wasn't easy
But after you leaving me that night to fend for myself
Is when I realised that if I couldn't save you
Nobody could."

"Don't let him take
The joy out of your smile
Baby girl, don't let him."

"Be unapologetic about who you are
What you love and believe in
People are going to talk about you regardless
And people aren't going to like you either
But guess who's problem that is? *Not yours.*"

"You'll search for me again
But by then I will already be gone
He would have already
Taken me away because soon
It'll be time for me to go home."

Miriama

"I hope you never know what it's like
To lose yourself to someone else."

"If there's one thing I hope to achieve
It's reaching the hearts of people around the world
Through words but not just any words
My words
The same words that bleed from old wounds
The same words I used when I screamed at the moon
The same words I wrote when I was fifteen
And I was tired of living
The same words I wrote when I turned twenty one
And I was thankful to be alive
Because if there's one thing I hope to achieve
It's letting people know that it really does
Get easier because it's one thing I know for sure
Is that it certainly doesn't seem like it at first
Then one day you wake up and it doesn't hit you
As hard as it used to
The pain no longer arrives at your doorstep
Moving towards you in a tidal wave
I hope to achieve and help you believe
That there comes a day where you wake up
And you finally feel like you are safe
There comes a day where you finally feel like yourself
One day you wake up and instead of begging
To the skies for them to let you die
You look up and you whisper that you are thankful
To still be alive and for once in your life, *you are*
So if there is anything that I hope to achieve
It's the hope that I can be the light
To guide everyone through the tunnel
Where we will all meet
At the other end, on the other side of pain
Promise, you'll meet me there?"

Miriama

"We all want to help each other
And be there for one another but
Sometimes the help we wish to *give*
Is not what wants to be *received*
On the other end."

"Friendly reminder;

You are brave
You are strong
You are powerful
You are beautiful
You can do this
You can achieve this
You can accomplish
Your goals
You are going places in your life
You are going to be amazing at this
You are going to make everyone proud

I believe in you
I am proud of you
I will always support you
I will always be here for you."

Miriama

"Know your worth
And don't let anyone tell you any different
You are beautiful, in every way
Beauty comes easy for someone like you
Don't forget this
Your kindness is the vibe you carry with you
On your shoulders
Not everyone knows what it's like
To be strong enough to carry what feels like
The weight of the world
But you do
You will get through this
You have to
Because the world needs someone like you
Even though you've never truly felt it
That doesn't stop you from spreading love
And positivity
Your feelings and experiences
Do not define who you are as a person
Neither do the mistakes you've made
Or the things you've said
You are everything that we need in this world
Be proud of how far you've come
This is all you, you did this
You did it."

"Keep going
Keep shining
Keep fighting
You can do this
You got this
I believe in you."

Miriama

"Don't feel guilty
For feeling proud of yourself."

"It's amazing what a little self-love can do for the soul
Trust me, I know."

"Even when my life has been crumbling to pieces
Literally crumbling to pieces
Remember that if you ever need me, *I'll be there*
Even when everything feels wrong in my life
I will always do the right thing and be there for you
But please do not mistake my kindness for weakness
If what I do for you is not given back to me
Then I cannot afford to stay and must instead leave
As for far too long, I have put in more than others
And for just once in my life
I would like to be cared for more than I care for."

"It isn't your fault that he left
He made that decision all on his own
You tried to convince him to stay
But he didn't want to listen
He has ears, *darling he heard you*
Crying and sobbing, begging
For him to not leave you
And if that itself
Did not break his heart
Then I don't know what will
I hope you see the truth in this
And I hope to God
That you are happy."

Miriama

"You all have the opportunity
To be happy but the question is
Are you going to take it?"

"When you learn self-love
And learn to fall in love with yourself
You realise that you don't need
Anyone else's validation
You also realise that you *never* did."

"Preserve the goodness that you have left over
Even after all the heartache and heartbreak
You are still you only *stronger, better, wiser*
Remain kind even when those you loved
Were not always kind to you."

"Protect your energy
It's yours for life
Remember that
There are very few
Who deserve
To be near it."

Miriama

"Be gentle with me
But don't be too careful with me."

"I hope that when your wife births a daughter for you
It helps you see the world from a woman's eyes
I hope it helps you realise what lies can do
To ones smile and I hope it helps you see
What late nights and early mornings
Have done to the mind of her mother
I hope you see everything clearly and I hope
You realise that she could've left you
Lonely and by yourself with nothing but didn't
I hope the birth of a daughter grants you
With the ability to understand women
And what they go through and I hope
Your daughter never has to feel the way
Her mother has ever felt before
Based on the mistakes of a man who just doesn't know
Any better than you once did."

Miriama

"We have been reformed
We have been renewed
And given a second chance
Let it be the last time
We need one
And let it be fucking glorious."

"I've heard of this flower
That grows in the darkness
I've heard that it blooms
Even in the shade and
Despite the darkness
This flower, she grows
And to be honest
I've never really thought
Of myself as a flower
But even in darkness and
Even in the shade
I have bloomed and grown
Despite what anyone else
Has ever said about me
Because I know my truth
My worth, my own value
And nothing that anyone
Has to say about me
Is ever going to destroy me
And anyone who tries
Will be shown
That even I can grow
From darkness and shade."

Miriama

"For my best friend, this is for you… thank you
Thank you for listening to me when no one else did
Thank you for believing in me when no one else did
Thank you for being there
Through everything that's happened in the last few years
Thank you for supporting every and any decision
And choice that I've ever made since knowing you
Even when you didn't agree with what I was doing
You still stuck by me through it all
Thank you for trusting me to make the right decisions
For myself even when you had your own doubts
Thank you for the undying and unconditional
Support and love that you have shown towards me
Thank you for telling me what I need to hear
And never what I've wanted to hear
Thank you for knowing what is best for me and always
Being there to show me the way when I cannot see
Thank you for all the things you've done for me
Thank you for allowing me
To be unapologetic about who I am and what I'm about
All while accepting me entirely as a person
I'm not sure what I did to deserve you but whatever it is
I'm so grateful because I don't know what I'd do
Without you and I don't think I'd even be here
If it weren't for you and I promise
That I will always be here for you to help you see
What I see when I look at you
I will never leave you and I will never let you believe
That you are alone and I won't ever let you think
That you don't have anyone to turn towards for help
And no matter what happens
You will always know where to find me
Whenever you need me."

"All the love I had for you
I turned into love for myself
Out of the two of us
I was the one who deserved it
More than you ever could."

Miriama

"There is hope in your eyes
And that is all I need to know
That you and I will be alright."

"Have hope
Have faith
You will get through
You'll make it out
On the other side
This troublesome feeling
Will not last forever
But the love in your heart
Surely will."

Miriama

"You have your entire life ahead of you
Don't spend your early teens trying to figure it all out
Live in the moment and be okay
With not knowing what's coming next
Because whatever it is
I promise that it'll be great."

"If you ever have to choose between
Being with someone and sacrificing
Something you love, choose yourself
And what you love because
Anyone who loves you will never think
Of making you choose between the two
Choose yourself, live for yourself
If the person you want to be with
Cannot respect you enough as a person
To allow you to have your own mind
They don't deserve anymore of your time."

Miriama

"I'm not perfect
But I love myself enough
That I could be."

"Learn to love yourself
Completely, entirely, fully
From head to toe
Because there is no love
In this entire world
That could ever replace
The love of self
The importance of it
Is deeply underestimated
And it shouldn't be so
Make yourself a priority."

Miriama

"If someone deserves you
They aren't going to do anything
That could jeopardise
Your feelings, remember that."

"Learn to forgive yourself
The sooner you learn to forgive yourself
The sooner you can learn to forgive others
And forgiveness is such a powerful trait to have
Not everyone is capable of it but you can be."

Miriama

"I don't think I love myself enough yet
To completely forgive myself
For the things that I have done in the past
That have hurt me and others
Along the way but I'm working on it
Slowly but surely, I'm getting there."

"Know your worth
Because believe it or not
In life there are going to be people
Who try to tarnish your name
And reputation
But at the end of the day
It doesn't matter as long as
You know the truth
About who you are and
Where you come from
Nothing anyone else says or thinks
About you will ever matter."

Miriama

TRUTHS

"No matter how deep
You try to bury
The truth
It will always
Always
Find its way
To the surface."

"Pressured into kissing boys
I didn't like
Afraid of being called a *prude*
But this game of theirs
Is only built for boys
And it only made me a *whore.*"

"I guess society still doesn't understand
That rape will last a few minutes for the rapist
But a lifetime for the victim
It is always there, *forever*."

Miriama

"Girl code
Learn it
Live by it
Die by it
Girl code."

"Why has society normalised teaching women
And young girls how to *not* get raped
And yet hasn't done anything about teaching
Men and young boys on how *not* to rape
Is this the world we live in now?"

Miriama

"Public service announcement from society, aimed at women;

Don't wear this, don't wear that
It's too short, it shows your shoulders too much
Don't smile too much or laugh too loud
If he thinks you like him then he'll think he owns you
And if you laugh at his jokes, he probably does
Don't entertain him if you're not interested
In having sex with him, he might get the wrong idea
If he gets the wrong idea about where he stands with you
Anything that happens after that is your fault
Don't let him buy you drinks and if you do
And you get drunk and something happens
Guess who's fault it is? Not his
Because why would you accept drinks from someone
You're not interested in having sex with?
Why would you wear all that makeup around him
And not expect him to make a move on you
If you think you're brave enough to come forward
Just remember that all of society have a responsibility
To protect you but we don't follow the rules
Instead we will protect the person you're accusing
We will claim that you are only an attention seeking whore
It will ruin your reputation, no one will like you
And even more so just know that no one will believe you
We will completely disregard the fact that you have proof
We will overpower you and make it all go away
The pain you feel is irrelevant to us and it will be with you
For the rest of your life but that's your responsibility
Not ours and if you had just followed our rules
Like you were supposed to then maybe
Just maybe this wouldn't have happened to you
Don't blame us, blame yourself
You're the one that didn't listen to us when we told you
What would happen...

Don't ask why we don't come forward and report
This is why, this says it all."

"Rape culture is real
And if you think otherwise
You can get the fuck up
And out of my life."

"Saying *no* means nothing these days
So think of it this way
Let's just pretend that *no*
Is short for *go away*
And if that doesn't make you understand
We can pretend it's short for
Fuck off."

"My daughters
And their daughters
Will know
How to scream *no*
And mean it
Regardless
Of love or privilege
No man or boy
Will ever
Feel capable
Of making her
Do anything
She already
Does not
Want to do."

Miriama

"It's simple
Don't expect respect
If you disrespect."

"It's a difficult lesson but a need-to-know
When it comes to others having the same heart as you
No matter how good you are towards someone else
They may not always be the same back."

Miriama

"I still don't know what I did to you
To deserve what you did to me."

"I cared about you, enough to stay through all the bullshit
You put me through but it didn't take you long to move on
I guess it was true when you said that you'd never cared
It was my fault for not believing in your truths
But how could you expect me to? When all you did was lie
And maybe it was fucked up of me to do what I did to you
I guess you still don't realise the reason why I acted like this
You pushed me away further and further and then
Had the nerve to sit there and accuse me of leaving you
You gave me no other choice, no other option
But it's okay because without you, I'm a better person
And surprisingly enough, I'm a happier person
This might surprise you because you think
That I was only ever happy because of you, due to you
But in fact, you're wrong, I can't remember a single time
You made me feel happy and if that doesn't say much
About me then it shows a heck of a lot about you in my eyes
I doubt you'd even remember what my eyes look like
It was always typical of you to act differently with me
Than anybody else, maybe there's something wrong with me
But if there's something wrong with me then there sure is
Something wrong with you too, who does this kind of thing
To people who genuinely care
Maybe I'll never know and maybe I don't ever want to
But I did care about you and that's something
I'll regret forever, it was never worth it."

Miriama

"Who do you think you are?
Looking at me with eyes that are both hungry and thirsty
At the same time
Who do you think you are?
As your eyes glide over my body, picking me apart
Limb by limb, one by one
Who do you think you are?
To act as if I am a beautiful painting hanging on the wall
Of an art gallery among many other beautiful paintings
You admire me and you admire the others
Then you tear me off the wall when you decide
That I am not as beautiful as the woman beside me
Your eyes are no longer hungry
Your eyes are no longer thirsty
Instead your reaction is that of someone who is
Indeed disgusted by what you see
Who do you think you are?
To mock me of my body, to poke fun
At the way my thighs come together when I sit down
To eat a burger and fries
Is this why you don't like me anymore?
Is this why you don't find me attractive anymore?
Is it the way my thighs connect that disrupts
The anger that you hold within yourself
Does this make you mad?
That you no longer have a way to get between my legs
Who do you think you are?
To whistle and call out derogatory names
To the woman across the road from you only
To get mad when another man has the same reaction
To your daughter, to your wife, to your sister
And to your mother
The next time you think about staring a woman down or
The next time you think about whistling and calling out
Think of your daughter
Think of your wife
Think of your sister
And think of your mother
What would you do if a man tried this on
With anyone of them?

Now imagine having that done
To you
Because that's what will happen
If you try and fuck with me again."

Miriama

"Stop apologising for the way
Others make you feel
Based on their actions or words
You don't owe them an apology
They owe you one."

"I thought I was ready
To open up, to share my story
I never knew how wrong
I could be until I tried
To come out into the world
As a survivor and not a victim
Society has a way
Of putting people like me
Back in their place…"

Miriama

"Sometimes it's hard to be happy
For people who only make you sad."

"Too young to be this broken
Too young to be this sad
Too goddamn young
And yet, here we are
Young, broken and sad."

Miriama

"The only person that can make a change
In your life is you
It all has to start and end with you
You're the one that calls the shots
And you get to decide what happens to you
And what happens in your life
So learn to trust yourself more
Deep down, you know what you're doing."

"Do your best to always do
What is best for you
Regardless of what others think
Or say about you
It's your life
They have their own to live
You have yours to live
So live it."

Miriama

"Know your worth
Because no matter what
You deserve the best."

"Anything you have done in the past
Does not define who you will become
In the future or who you are right now
In the present and anyone who thinks
They can try and make you out to be
Someone you're not is someone who
Doesn't deserve to be anywhere near you."

Miriama

"I'm sorry to anyone I hurt or have hurt before
I'm sorry to anyone who needs me and I can't be there
For you efficiently to make sure that you get through
And I'm sorry to my family
For doing everything differently that it's gotten me
Somewhat behind in life and this isn't the way
I thought my life was going to be either
And some days I really wish it wasn't like this
But it is so right now all I'm hoping for is to get by
All I want is to get through to the next day and be okay."

"Don't promise to be different
Then turn out to be exactly the same."

"I can and will
Always love you
But respecting you
As a person
As a human being
Is not possible
Because you have
Never respected me
As a person
As a human being."

"You judged me
Before you even knew me
Now sit back
And watch me strive
Because this time
I'm reaching for the stars."

Miriama

"You cannot possibly expect to be able
To make everyone in your life happy
And you shouldn't even try to
Because at the end of the day
You have to do what's best for you
If the people in your life don't agree
Or don't like what you decide to do
Then that's their own decision
But you shouldn't feel like you have to
Live your life to the best of *their* abilities
And you should just simply
Live your life to the best of *your* abilities."

"This is your life
You are living your own life
Who is anyone else to tell you how to do it?"

Miriama

"It's sad how quickly
People will drop things they love
For someone they love
No one who loves you enough
Will ever make you
Pick and choose
What you do and don't do
In your own life."

"A gentle reminder
That it's okay to take days off to care for yourself
Love yourself and be there for yourself
The world will continue to go on
And the earth will keep spinning
The sun will still rise in the morning and keep shining
The moon will visit again as darkness falls
And the stars will bring light to the night sky
You are allowed to take a day or two or more
To fend for yourself
Because how could you think that you can help others
If you can't even help yourself
There is nothing wrong with putting yourself first
Or wanting the best for yourself
A gentle reminder to the reader
And a gentle reminder for the writer."

Miriama

"Do not let society
Store you in a box
Afraid that you will say
Things they cannot admit
Use the voice that He gave you
For good and don't ever be scared
To tell it like it is."

"All I can think about is how I can't take your pain away
And it breaks my heart each and every day."

Miriama

"You tell me you're tired
But your voice tells me
You're broken."

"I hope you find a way
To believe in yourself
Because you matter."

Miriama

"I accepted the truth
Because you gave me
No other option, I had to."

"Hiding from the truth
Doesn't make it go away."

Miriama

"Violence
Should never
Ever be an option
Neither should
Aggression
Stop allowing
This shit
To happen."

"Friendships end
Relationships end
They tell you
That all good things
Will eventually
Come to an end
But I couldn't let go
I don't want to let go."

Miriama

"Another victim
Of creation
Trying to outlive
What society
Has deemed of me."

"I still don't understand
How someone can possibly be
This blatantly ignorant
In their own blissful
Arrogance."

Miriama

"I probably wouldn't feel this way
If you had listened to me the first time."

"Stay away from people
Who would rather blame you
Than own up to their own faults."

Miriama

"If they want to be with you
They will show you
They wouldn't let a day go by
Without letting you know
How they feel about you
And the beautiful thing about it
Is you get the opportunity
To do the same thing for them
And that my friends
Is reciprocation
And it's important
If you didn't know that before
I hope you realise it now."

"When I said forever
I meant it
When you said forever
You lied."

Miriama

"Sometimes even the people
We once considered friends
Are capable of turning
Into the people we hate the most."

"Hate is a strong word
And I don't like to use it
What people don't get is
Love is a strong word too
Yet people throw it around
Like it means *nothing*
When it means *everything*."

Miriama

"You wanted me to let my walls down
And that's exactly what I did
You wanted me to let you in and so I did
But even though I did all of this for you
You weren't able to do the same for me
And that's what hurt the most."

"Just know that *moving on*
Doesn't necessarily mean
Getting into another relationship
Sometimes moving on
Is doing what it takes
To move forward with your life
Even if it hurts."

Miriama

"It's clear now
I would've been better off
If I had just sold my soul
Because loving you
Felt way worse."

"I should've known
That someone like me
Does not end up
With someone like you."

"And the truth is, I don't have my shit together
I'm not even sure when I will or if I ever will
But right now, I'm happy
Right now, I'm living and I'm breathing
I'm still here and right now
That's all that matters to me."

"The future itself
Depends on women
Treat us kindly."

Miriama

"I was blessed
On the first day
That I arrived
Into this world
To have parents
Like the ones
I've got."

"Even though I could never hate you
I could never respect you either
But right now life is too short
For me to hold something
That you cannot control, against you."

"Sometimes I wish that I could redo everything
That ever happened between us
I wish for a do-over but at the end of the day
I would do it all over again and again
If it meant that this is where we would end up
I know it's been hard on us
And we've had more than a few difficulties
But I have faith in us and I always have
The ending of us was only the beginning
Look how far we've come since then
I can't wait for a life well spent with you
Whatever it may be, whatever happens
As long as you've got me, you'll be okay
And as long as I've got you, I'll be okay."

"Every time I think about the way I treated you
I just want to break down and cry
I try to think of all the reasons why and how
Someone could be so cruel, I was evil in a way but just know
I loved you so much it hurt
Except it hurt you more than it hurt me
It wasn't meant to be like this
I swear it wasn't but as of right now
I'm clueless and I've forgotten how to make it right
Late at night I'm awake just thinking
Of all the mistakes I made
Thinking of all the regrets I have
And all the things I've said in vain and spite
Just to cause you pain on purpose
I know you'll only say I broke your heart once
But I know the truth and I know it was more than that
And saying sorry and apologising won't do anything
You put your trust in me despite your instincts
Telling you otherwise and if I'm ever sorry
To anyone for anything, it's you and what I did
It's how I broke everything you gave me
I broke your love, I broke your trust
I broke your faith and I broke your heart
I broke your happiness, your mind and your soul
I broke the look in your eyes when you see me
It's not the same anymore and only I can see it
I know it's wrong of me to think
That you're the crazy one
When we all know for a fact that you ain't the only one
But out of the two of us, I'm the nut job
And you're the sane one
At least that's what you always say
I wish I could go back in time and change everything
But I can't and instead I will spend my life with you
Right by my side and I will make things right for us
You deserve the world and I will find a way
To serve it to you on a golden platter
I don't want to look back on the past anymore
Let's keep moving forward
The future is ours if we really want it."

"I didn't get lost in your eyes
I got lost in the lies that you sold me
That fed off the romantic fantasies
That I wanted fulfilled so badly
You ended me completely
You left me, alone and lost
With nothing more to give
Because you had already
Taken it all, I loved you
At least I thought I did but now
I look back and reminisce
Wondering if I ever really did
I guess in the end I started to fall in love
With the lies you told, the things you said
But it was never a part of my reality
It was never about the truth for you."

"I gave you all of me
And all I got in return
Were tiny, little pieces
Of you
And that's why
When I think of you
I think of you as
The thief of all things beautiful
Because that's what I was
Before I met you."

Miriama

"It's easier to accept the love we are used to
Than to believe that maybe, just maybe
We deserve more or better than what we have already
It's easier to accept the love we think we deserve
Rather than the love we should be receiving
And it's so easy to love someone who we know
Isn't good for us because we want them to change
Into who we need them to be
But it's the hardest thing to have to let go of someone
Who we feel is genuinely the one for us
But sometimes it has to be done."

"Loving someone is having the power to hurt them
And doing everything you can, not to
Being loved by someone
Is giving them the power to hurt you
And trusting them not to
So I hope I live long enough to love you forever
Because even when I'm gone
I will still love you and never hurt you."

Miriama

"I keep myself busy and distracted
As often as possible, every day if need be
Because I hate the feeling of you
On my mind
Memories of us play on repeat
I can't get you out, I can't sleep
I just want it all to stop but it never does
So instead I keep myself busy and distracted
For as long as I need because
I'm still too in love with you
But you don't want to be mine anymore
I'm just doing what I gotta do to get through."

"I still don't want to believe
That you would do this to me
I hate you but I love you
I just can't understand why
What did I do?"

Miriama

"I don't know what the truth is anymore
Maybe we're not destined to be together after all
Perhaps it's more like
We're doomed to be together instead."

"*Do you feel like you lie to me less?* He asks me
Yes, I lie."

"Maybe the truth is inevitable
Like death, like life
Maybe no matter what
The truth will always come out
It will always be revealed
Perhaps there's nowhere in the world
That you can try and hide it
But God knows, I will damn well try."

distorted colours and beautiful disasters

"Do you remember when you told me
That you don't know what love is
Do you remember what I told you
After I screamed at you to leave me alone
I told you that I've been standing
Right in front of you this entire time
And you've never so much as noticed me
Do you remember when you told me
That you don't love me anymore
Do you remember what I told you
After I cried out for you to come back
I told you that you've always loved me
But you just won't accept it
I told you that you can't accept that you love me
And I let you know that I don't know
What you expect me to do about it
Because I'm the one that's been here since day one
You just can't seem to see that
Do you remember how much it hurt you
When you left and I accepted it
Do you remember how much it pained you
That I did not beg for you to stay
Like all those other times
The reason why is simple and I'll explain it
If you cannot accept the love I give
Then I cannot accept you
If you cannot accept that you love me
Then I cannot accept you
You may not know what love is
But you damn sure know that I love you
And if you can't accept this then I cannot accept you
Because I've been here right in front of you
For years now and I need you to notice me
I just need you to fucking notice me."

Miriama

"I'm still exhausted
From all those nights
I would lay awake
Waiting for you
To come home."

distorted colours and beautiful disasters

"I know you mean well and you're not trying on purpose
To push me away but sometimes I wonder if
You're actually even here to stay or if it's because
You need the company to get through another day and
I know better than what I'm thinking but deep down
I'm always going to be afraid that you'll leave me again
After everything that's happened you and I both know
I've always had trouble accepting change but in order
For us to grow and become *stronger, better, wiser*
Than we have ever been before I need to look past
The past and move forward in the direction that looks
As if it could be a bright future for you and I but first
I need you to promise me that everything
Is going to be okay and I need you to tell me
That everything will be alright because I can't stand
The thought of losing you
Just like I told you when we started this once more
If you ever leave me like that again, you'll regret it
It's not a threat or a warning, it's just the truth
And you know it."

Miriama

"I want to be raw
Honest and truthful
Real and alive
But this only shows
In the way that I write
And not in real life."

"Don't let me regret
Anything I ever did
For you."

"Don't tell me I asked for it
Based on what I was wearing
Don't tell me I begged for it
Based on what I was saying
Don't ever try to convince me
That I did something to provoke
What he did to me
You know damn well, I didn't."

"Don't ask why victims don't come forward
Why would we?
We are already disregarded as seeking attention
Told that we did something or wore something
To provoke what happened to us and yet
The ones who do this to us are protected
By almost all of society
We are the ones who are accused of trying to ruin
Someone else's life and yet our lives
Are ruined and come to an end
Based on the actions of a man they wish to protect
I still don't understand how this is so *normal*."

Miriama

"I told my best friend what he did to me
She turned around and said to me
You asked for it, you wanted this
You're single, who cares?
He didn't rape you, he tried to
It's not the same, you got away
Even though that exact same day I said to her
I'm not interested
He knows, you know and I'll make sure
The whole world knows if I have to
She laughed and looked me in the face and said
He wouldn't do that, I know him
He isn't that type of person
Why are you trying to ruin his reputation?
I had to give up on pleading my case
Realising that nothing I could say
Was going to change her mind about him
And I knew if I continued talking about it
She would see me differently
But I soon came to know that it was too late
She already saw straight through me
I thought about coming forward with my pain
To others close to me but
If my own *best friend* at the time didn't believe me
Why would anyone else?"

"I couldn't say anything to anyone
If I did I would have been bombarded
With all these questions like
What were you wearing?
Were you drinking?
What did you do to give him the wrong idea?
Even if I had opened up about it
What would have happened?
He was everyone's favourite *life of the party*
Who would I be to take that away?"

"I just want you to know
That it was the relationship that ended
Not your life
And even after everything and everyone
Has gone away
You will still be here
You matter, you are important
Your life doesn't have to end
Just because a relationship in your life did
This is just something I wish I knew
When I was younger
I'm older and now I know the truth
So this is my message to you
Pick yourself up, you got this baby girl
I believe in you."

"You are everything
The world needs you to be
And so much more."

Miriama

"There's no right time to tell you this, no right words
To use when I speak on it but mama I found myself
In some trouble and I thought the people around me
Would have been the ones to stop it and protect me
Instead of leaving me behind and encouraging this
And dad, I know I should've come to you sooner but
I was scared and I didn't know how to share this
The pain of it all has caused me to become ashamed
And embarrassed at what happened to me
I still feel sick over it to this day and it hasn't yet
Been an entire year but I'm still trying to force myself
To be over it by now, I'm just trying to heal quickly
And my love; I wish I could find the words to tell you
I'm sorry for not telling you when it all happened
Just know that this has been the hardest thing
For me to go through, I've never felt so alone and
When I'm with you it's so easy to forget about it all
It's so easy to forget all the bad things that happened
To me and I hope I can make you understand
I hope I can make you see the truth and I guess
It scared me when she didn't believe me when I told her
Maybe that's why it's taken me so long
To come forward and be open with my pain and share
With the ones who actually care about me
I don't want any of you to think you failed me
I'm still trying to convince myself that I didn't do this
To myself and let this happen all on my own
The truth is, I'm trying to heal from this pain
And the healing process is ugly and lately
It's been driving me insane, I keep telling myself
That it wasn't my fault and I hope I hear the same words
From you all and that this isn't another mistake to add
To an already long list
I love you all and I hope your love for me doesn't change
Can't do this without you."

distorted colours and beautiful disasters

"Maybe the truth is that I don't know what I'm doing
And maybe you don't either and that's okay
Because perhaps that's what life is all about
I don't want to have everything figured out right now
And I don't want to live my life worried
That something bad is going to happen to me
Just because I don't have my shit together entirely
Like everyone else claims they do
I don't know what's going to happen tomorrow
And I don't know what's going to happen today
Or next week or next month or next year
Part of me hates not knowing things but
All I know is that I'm here and I'm going to
Continue being a part of this world
I'm going to continue striving to make a change
For myself, for those around me and others
I don't know what the future has in store for me
But the truth is that I'm going to be okay and
Everything is going to be alright
Maybe I just tell myself this to help me sleep at night
Either way, I'm here and I'm alive
That's all that matters to me right now
And that's the truth, that's my truth."

Miriama

;

ABOUT: the book

This book contains a collection of poetry that takes you through five chapters: *loss, pain, love, hope* and *truths*. I chose the names of these chapters based off what I have experienced in my own life, this is the result.

This is simply my way of setting myself free, I'm letting you all be a part of that and I am so thankful that you are all here with me to share this journey. I hope it makes sense to you as much as it does for me.

I hope it helps you more than it could ever help me. I hope it helps you more than I ever could.

ABOUT: the writer

There isn't really much to say about myself; I was fifteen when I decided that I was going to write a book, twenty when I finally figured out what I wanted it to contain and twenty one when I finished writing it and eventually published it.

I started sharing my writing on Instagram a little over a year ago, I still cannot grasp the amount of people that I have managed to reach through words. It still doesn't feel real but it is and I'm ready for this, ready for whatever comes my way.

It has been such an exhausting and yet wonderful but also eye-opening journey, I'm happy I have been able to experience and share it with all of you. Thank you for allowing me to share my story, my words, my writing; thank you letting me be *me*.

I can only hope that you are all able to enjoy what I have managed to put together. For me, for you; for us.

Sending all my love to you.

Sincerely,

Miri

For my Nanna;

Even though you're gone, it still feels like you're here. I miss you more and more with each passing day, I wish I could see you once more but even that will involve saying goodbye to you all over again. Instead I will wait until we meet again, I will wait for a time where saying goodbye won't even be an option. I know that day will come eventually; in the meantime, I will continue to do what I love and what I believe in. I will continue doing my best and not let anyone break me along the way, I want to make you proud and I think I've done well.

If I do this for anyone else and not just myself, it would all be for you. Thank you for encouraging me to put this out into the world, it hasn't been easy without you but I won't ever forget you and the life you brought to the party. Always missing you, always loving you.

Until we meet again.

Made in the USA
Columbia, SC
22 November 2019